TOO HOT TO HOOT

Other Clarion Word Play Books You'll Enjoy
by Marvin Terban
Illustrated by Giulio Maestro

I Think I Thought
And Other Tricky Verbs

In a Pickle
And Other Funny Idioms

Eight Ate
A Feast of Homonym Riddles

TOO HOT TO HOOT

FUNNY PALINDROME RIDDLES

by MARVIN TERBAN
illustrated by
GIULIO MAESTRO

CLARION BOOKS
New York

Clarion Books
a Houghton Mifflin Company imprint
215 Park Avenue South, New York, NY 10003
Text copyright © 1985 by Marvin Terban
Illustrations copyright © 1985 by Giulio Maestro
Printed in the USA

Library of Congress Cataloging in Publication Data
Terban, Marvin.
Too hot to hoot.

Summary: A collection of progressively harder to guess palindrome riddles.
1. Riddles, Juvenile.   2. Palindromes—Juvenile
literature.   [1. Palindromes.   2. Riddles]   I. Maestro,
Giulio, ill.   II. Title.
PN6371.5.T44   1985   818'.5402   84-14942
RNF ISBN 0-89919-319-6
PAP ISBN 0-89919-320-X

HOR 10 9 8 7 6 5

For Karen, Jennifer, and David
A MOM, a SIS, and a WOW of a son,
From DAD

Contents

Introduction

Did you ever hear of palindromes? You may be surprised to learn that you use some palindromes every day. It would be hard not to use them.

Palindromes are words or phrases that are spelled the same way backward as they are forward. People have been having fun making up palindromes for centuries. Now you can have fun trying to guess the answers to the humorous palindrome riddles in this book.

These palindrome riddles start easy, but watch out. They get trickier and trickier. From left to right or right to left, the palindromes, called "pals" for short, will have *you* coming and going.

You may want to have a pencil and paper handy to write down your answers in four of the six chapters. Then check them with the answer page at the end of those chapters. Good luck!

·1·

Three-Letter Palindrome Riddles

Here are some one-word, three-letter palindromes. Many are everyday words. Remember, the answers are the same backward or forward. Try to guess the answers first. Then check them with the answer page at the end of this chapter.

What's a three-letter word for...

1. mother

2. father

3. small child

4. energy

5. joke

YUMBONE

6. little dog

And what's a three-letter word for...

7. short for Robert

8. Today I do.
   Yesterday I __?__

9. girl relative of brother

10. sudden, sharp,
    explosive sound

11. boy Pharaoh,
    King ___?___

12. a firecracker that
    doesn't explode

Here are some tougher three-letter "pals."

13. exclamation of
    confusion

14. exclamation of great
    wonder or surprise

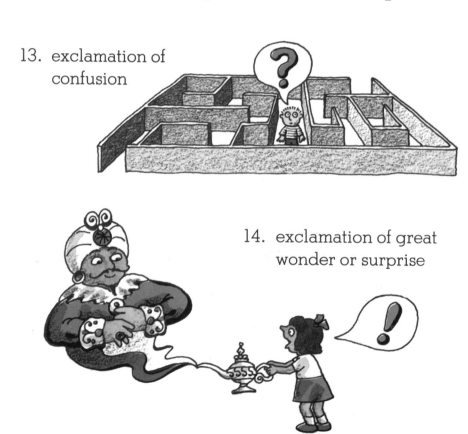

15. famous lady of
    the 1800s,
    Diamond ___?___

16. an explosive:
    trinitrotoluene

17. a two-wheeled,
    horse-drawn carriage

18. what a British child
    calls his mother

19. baby's clothes protector

20. soft food for babies

21. seed of a fruit; dot
    on dice

22. distress signal

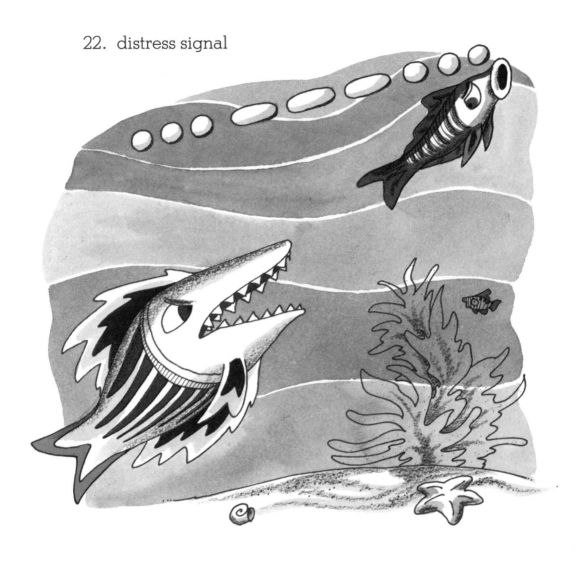

23. a religious woman

24. to make lace

Here are more three-letter palindromes. Some are not so common. Each word begins and ends with the letter e.

1. the first woman on earth

2. what you see with

3. to barely manage to make a living

4. a female sheep

5. an old-fashioned word for *before*

ANSWERS TO THE
THREE-LETTER PALINDROMES

Pages 11 to 17

1.	MOM	19.	BIB
2.	DAD	20.	PAP
3.	TOT	21.	PIP
4.	PEP	22.	SOS
5.	GAG	23.	NUN
6.	PUP	24.	TAT
7.	BOB		
8.	DID	Pages 18 to 19	
9.	SIS	1.	EVE
10.	POP	2.	EYE
11.	TUT	3.	EKE
12.	DUD	4.	EWE
13.	HUH	5.	ERE
14.	WOW		
15.	LIL		
16.	TNT		
17.	GIG		
18.	MUM		

· 2 ·

Getting Trickier

Now it's time for palindrome words of four, five, and more letters. Hint: Numbers 1 to 4 have oo in the middle; numbers 5 to 7 have ee in the middle.

Four-letter Palindromes

1. 12:00 in the daytime

2. a really peculiar person (slang)

3. deck above the main deck of a ship

4. sound of a boat horn

5. a paper that shows you own property

6. sound of a young bird

7. looks at

8. short for *Madam*

9. an all-right knockout

Five-letter Palindromes

1. an Eskimo canoe

2. part of a machine that turns or rotates

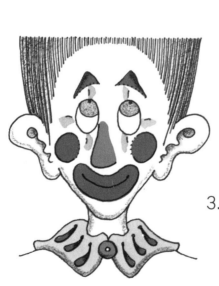

3. having a flat, even surface

4. males and females

5. referring to a city, citizens, or citizenship

6. performances done by one person alone

7. former rulers of Iran

8. to make reference to

9. <u>ra</u>dio <u>d</u>etecting <u>an</u>d <u>r</u>anging device

10. long adventure stories about heroes

11. long for *Ma'am*

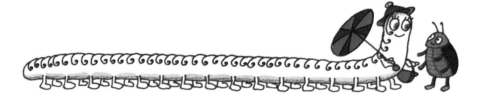

More Than Five Letters

1. If you put more red in, you make the color ___?___

2. What do you call the person who brings someone back to life or consciousness?

3. What do you do when you put wallpaper up again?

More Than One Word

Are you ready for some really challenging riddle "pals"? Think carefully and try to guess these.

1. What is 1,999½ pounds?

2. What do owners of a company do when business goes bad?

3. What does a boy not want his father to say?

4. When a patient needs help in a hurry, what do the women in white do?

5. What do wise men run their cars on?

6. What do we dressmakers do?

7. On a menu, what are sweets that are emphasized?

ANSWERS TO THE GETTING TRICKIER PALINDROMES

Pages 12 to 25
1. NOON
2. KOOK
3. POOP
4. TOOT
5. DEED
6. PEEP
7. SEES
8. MA'AM
9. OK KO

Pages 26 to 28
1. KAYAK
2. ROTOR
3. LEVEL
4. SEXES
5. CIVIC
6. SOLOS
7. SHAHS
8. REFER
9. RADAR
10. SAGAS
11. MADAM

Page 29
1. REDDER
2. REVIVER
3. REPAPER

Pages 30 to 31
1. NOT A TON
2. BOSSES SOB
3. NO, SON
4. NURSES RUN
5. SAGES USE GAS
6. WE SEW
7. STRESSED DESSERTS

·3·

Flip-Flop Phrases

There are many words that, when spelled backward, become other words. For example, *tub* backward is *but*, and *raw* backward is *war*. Let's call them flip-flop words.

If you put two flip-flop words together, you have a flip-flop phrase. For instance, *sub* and *bus* are flip-flop words. The phrase *sub bus* could be the answer to the riddle, "What is an underwater vehicle with many seats?"

See if you can guess the flip-flop phrase answers to the following riddles. REMEMBER, YOU CAN READ THESE PHRASES BACKWARD OR FORWARD, AND THEY'RE STILL THE SAME.

How Do You Say...

1. cooking utensil lid

2. snuggly friend

3. canine deity

4. heavy cup to hold chewing sticks

5. swine swindle

Valuable GIFT Inside!

6. gossipy paper container

7. cold water fish physician

8. very angry water barrier

9. basketball hoop after #9

10. top edge of ditch

11. pistols that are tight in their holsters

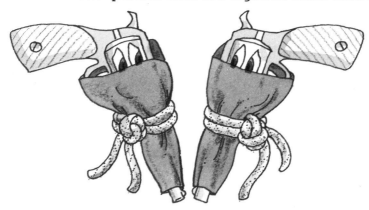

12. Who have the leads in the rodents' variety show?

13. When animals trade in their hands, they
    __?__ __?__.

14. when friends strike each other

15. "Gently touch Patricia."

16. "I lost then, but I __?__ __?__."

17. "Sleep, metal frying dish."

18. scarecrow's skin lumps

19. what the devil wants you to do

20. household animal's stair

21. What spoiled the artist's painting?

ANSWERS TO THE FLIP-FLOP PHRASES

Pages 34 to 39

1. POT TOP		12. RATS STAR
2. LAP PAL		13. SWAP PAWS
3. DOG GOD		14. PALS SLAP
4. GUM MUG		15. TAP PAT
5. PIG GIP		16. WON NOW
6. GAB BAG		17. NAP, PAN
7. COD DOC		18. STRAW WARTS
8. MAD DAM		19. LIVE EVIL
9. NET TEN		20. PET'S STEP
10. PIT TIP		21. BAD DAB
11. SNUG GUNS		

·4·

Palindrome Sentences

Now we're ready for full-length palindromic sentences. These are tough. Note: Punctuation does not count.

Read these two sentences forward and backward *word by word*, not letter by letter.

KING, ARE YOU GLAD YOU ARE KING?

YOU CAN CAGE A SWALLOW, CAN'T YOU, BUT YOU CAN'T SWALLOW A CAGE, CAN YOU?

Now that you've got the idea of palindromic sentences, read the rest of these backward and forward *letter by letter*. There will be different spacing between the letters when you read the sentence backward.

"FLEE TO ME, REMOTE ELF."

"FLE ETOMER EM OT EELF"

1.

TOO HOT TO HOOT

2.

"CIGAR? TOSS IT IN A CAN. IT IS SO TRAGIC."

3.

"A TIN MUG FOR A JAR OF GUM, NITA?"

4.

MA HANDED EDNA HAM.

5.

"RED RUM, SIR, IS MURDER."

6.

DELIA SAILED. EVA WAVED. ELIAS AILED.

7.

"DID HANNAH SAY AS HANNAH DID?"

8.

ENID AND EDNA DINE.

9.

"LEW, OTTO HAS A HOT TOWEL."

10.

"NAOMI, DID I MOAN?"

11.

"NIAGARA, O ROAR AGAIN!"

12.

NO LEMONS. NO MELON.

13.

NOT NEW YORK. ROY WENT ON.

14.

"NOW, SIR, A WAR IS WON!"

15.

"OH, WHO WAS IT I SAW? OH, WHO?"

16.

PAT AND EDNA TAP.

17.

POOR DAN IS IN A DROOP.

18.

"PULL UP, EVA! WE'RE HERE! WAVE! PULL UP!"

19.

"RISE TO VOTE, SIR."

20.

"ROY, AM I MAYOR?"

21.

STEP ON NO PETS

22.

"TOO BAD I HID A BOOT."

23.

"WAS IT A RAT I SAW?"
"NO, MISS. IT IS SIMON."

24.

"PULL UP IF I PULL UP."

25.

A DOG! A PANIC IN A PAGODA!

26.

"WAS IT A CAR OR A CAT I SAW?"

27.

"SH! TOM SEES MOTHS."

28.

"WE'LL LET DAD TELL LEW."

29.

"YAWN A MORE ROMAN WAY."

30.

"EUSTON SAW I WAS NOT SUE."

31.

"DID DEAN AID DIANA?" "ED DID."

32.

"NO MISSES ORDERED ROSES, SIMON."

33.

MARGE LETS NORAH SEE SHARON'S TELEGRAM.

34.

"DRAW, O COWARD!"

35.

"NEVER ODD OR EVEN."

36.

"PUPILS!" I SAY AS I SLIP UP.

·5·

Palindromic Numbers

Numbers, not just words and letters, can be arranged to read the same backward and forward.

Think of years. In the last thousand years, one year each century was a palindrome:

1001	1331	1661
1111	1441	1771
1221	1551	1881

What will the next two palindromic years be?

If you write out full dates in numbers, you'll discover that some dates are the same backward and forward. For instance, January 4, 1941, written out in numbers is 1/4/41.

What are the palindromic numbers for these dates?

1. February 8, 1982
2. March 23, 1923
3. April 1, 1914
4. May 20, 1925
5. June 30, 1936
6. July 31, 1937

7. August 1, 1918
8. September 8, 1989
9. October 1, 1901
10. November 5, 1911
11. December 11, 1921

Amazingly, at least once each decade, there is a perfect palindromic date. It's perfect because nothing could be more palindromic than the same number repeated. It reads perfectly backward and forward. What are these dates for the twentieth century?

12. January 1, 1911
13. February 2, 1922
14. March 3, 1933
15. April 4, 1944
16. May 5, 1955

17. June 6, 1966
18. July 7, 1977
19. August 8, 1988
20. September 9, 1999

Actually, 1911 had four palindromic dates, January 1 and 11, and November 1 and 11. The year 1922 had two such dates, February 2 and 22.

What will be the palindromic dates in the twenty-first century? The answer may surprise you.

Addition Magic

Think of a number with two digits like 13. Reverse the two digits—31. Add the numbers.

$$
\begin{array}{rl}
13 & \text{number} \\
+31 & \text{reverse} \\
\hline
44 & \text{palindrome}
\end{array}
$$

The answer is often a palindromic number.

Sometimes it takes two steps:

$$
\begin{array}{rl}
28 & \text{number} \\
+82 & \text{reverse} \\
\hline
110 & \text{sum} \\
+011 & \text{reverse} \\
\hline
121 & \text{palindrome}
\end{array}
$$

Sometimes it takes four steps to reach the palindromic sum.

$$
\begin{array}{r}
789 \\
+\,987 \\
\hline
\end{array}
\quad
\begin{array}{l}
\text{number} \\
\text{reverse}
\end{array}
$$

$$
\begin{array}{r}
1776 \\
+\,6771 \\
\hline
\end{array}
\quad
\begin{array}{l}
\text{sum} \\
\text{reverse}
\end{array}
$$

$$
\begin{array}{r}
8547 \\
+\,7458 \\
\hline
\end{array}
\quad
\begin{array}{l}
\text{sum} \\
\text{reverse}
\end{array}
$$

$$
\begin{array}{r}
16005 \\
+\,50061 \\
\hline
\end{array}
\quad
\begin{array}{l}
\text{sum} \\
\text{reverse}
\end{array}
$$

$$
\begin{array}{r}
66066
\end{array}
\quad \text{palindrome}
$$

Try finding palindromic numbers on your own, but be prepared to do a lot of adding. The eventual palindrome of 56814 is 56677665, and it takes seven addition steps to reach. Your calculator may give up after twelve steps when trying to reach the palindrome of 89. And you'd better get a year's supply of fresh batteries if you try to find the palindrome of 196. You'll have to reverse, add, reverse, add, reverse, add 4,147 times!!

ANSWERS TO THE PALINDROMIC NUMBERS

Page 54
The next two palindromic years will be 1991 and 2002.

Page 55

1.	2/8/82	12.	1/1/11
2.	3/23/23	13.	2/2/22
3.	4/1/14	14.	3/3/33
4.	5/20/25	15.	4/4/44
5.	6/30/36	16.	5/5/55
6.	7/31/37	17.	6/6/66
7.	8/1/18	18.	7/7/77
8.	9/8/89	19.	8/8/88
9.	10/1/01	20.	9/9/99
10.	11/5/11		
11.	12/11/21		

The perfect palindromic dates in the twenty-first century will be exactly the same as those in this century. That's because when we write out a date in numbers, we never include the century. For instance, March 3, 2033, will be written 3/3/33.

•6•

Three Famous Palindromes

Here are the stories behind the three best-known palindrome sentences ever created.

The first is about Theodore Roosevelt (1858–1919), the twenty-sixth president of the United States (from 1901 to 1909). He felt that one of his most important accomplishments as president was getting the Panama Canal dug in Central America in the early 1900s. The canal greatly shortened shipping time from the Atlantic to the Pacific Ocean. A palindromic wiz once said about President Roosevelt:

"A MAN, A PLAN, A CANAL—PANAMA!"

THIS WAY TO
The Panamanian
Shortcut

Napoleon Bonaparte, the emperor of France from 1804 to 1815, was a powerful military leader who had dreams of great conquest. He won many important battles, but he was defeated at the Battle of the Nations in 1813. He abdicated his throne and was exiled to the island of Elba in the Mediterranean Sea.

If Napoleon spoke English and talked in palindromes, you could imagine him on Elba commenting on his lost powers like this:

"ABLE WAS I ERE I SAW ELBA."

By the way, Napoleon escaped from Elba, returned to France, and became emperor again for about one hundred more days. He tried to fight again against European countries, was defeated at the Battle of Waterloo in Belgium in 1815, was deported to another island, and died there in 1821.

We can imagine another famous person, the world's first man, Adam, uttering the following famous palindrome sentence when meeting the world's first woman in the Garden of Eden:

"MADAM, I'M ADAM."

If the woman thought he was crazy, a slight shift of the spacing would have changed the meaning of the palindrome entirely:

"MAD? AM I, MADAM?"

If Adam were a bit more talkative, he could have included his location in his palindromic introduction:

"MADAM, IN EDEN I'M ADAM."

Being polite, the woman could have introduced herself with the perfect one-word palindrome mentioned earlier in this book:

"EVE."

AUTHOR'S NOTE

If you'd like to read more about palindromes, you might want to get the following two books that I used in my research for this book:

Palindromes and Anagrams by Howard W. Bergeson, Dover Publications, Inc., New York, 1973

and

Language on Vacation by Dmitri A. Borgmann, Charles Scribner's Sons, New York, 1965.

Special thanks to my dear friend Edward Siegel, whose love of language, word play, and the well-turned phrase inspired me to write this book.

ABOUT THE AUTHOR

Too Hot to Hoot is Marvin Terban's fourth word play book for Clarion. Mr. Terban teaches at Columbia Grammar and Preparatory School in Manhattan where he delights his students by finding new ways to teach English. He also directs children's plays during the summer at Cejwin Camps in Port Jervis, New York. Mr. Terban lives in New York City with his wife Karen, a teacher, their two children, and a cat.

ABOUT THE ARTIST

Giulio Maestro has illustrated many books for children including four by Marvin Terban. He has also written and illustrated two riddle books of his own for Clarion. Mr. Maestro lives in Madison, Connecticut, with his wife Betsy, a writer, and their two children.